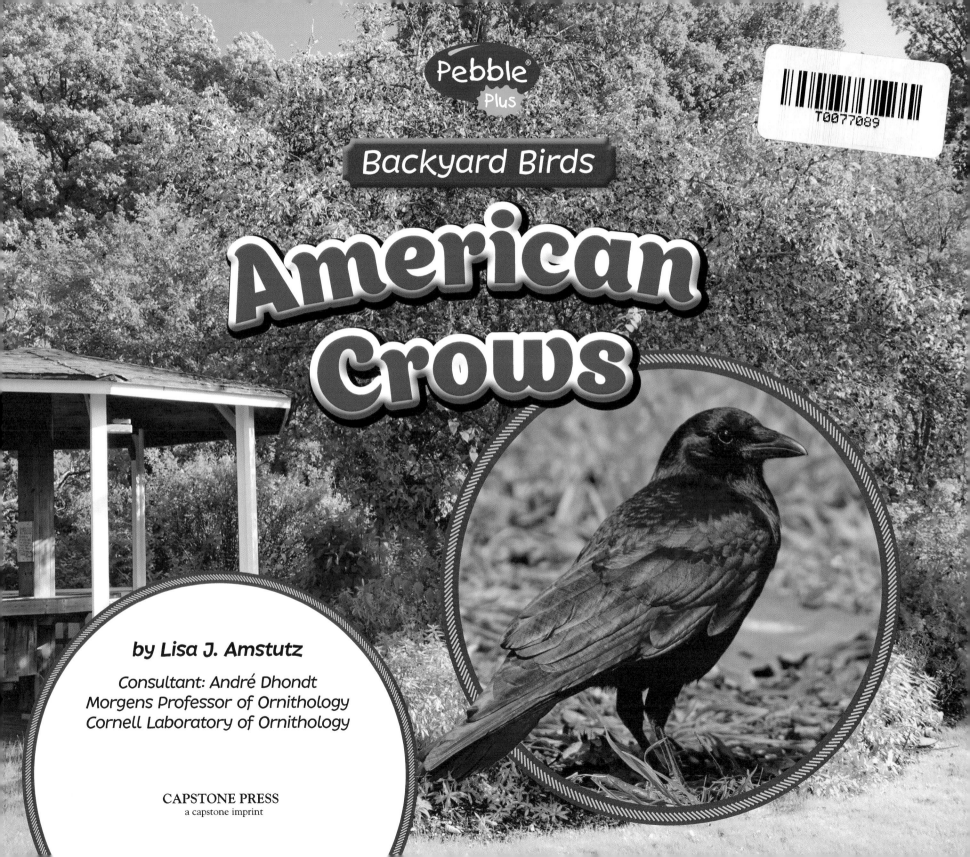

Pebble® Plus

Backyard Birds

American Crows

by Lisa J. Amstutz

Consultant: André Dhondt
Morgens Professor of Ornithology
Cornell Laboratory of Ornithology

CAPSTONE PRESS
a capstone imprint

T0077089

Pebble Plus is published by Capstone Press,
1710 Roe Crest Drive, North Mankato, Minnesota 56003
www.mycapstone.com

Library of Congress Cataloging-in-Publication Data
Amstutz, Lisa J.
American crows / by Lisa J. Amstutz.
    pages cm. -- (Backyard birds)
Includes bibliographical references and index.
Audience: Ages 5 to 7.
Audience: Grades K to 3.
ISBN 978-1-4914-8511-8 (library binding)
ISBN 978-1-4914-8515-6 (paperback)
ISBN 978-1-4914-8519-4 (eBook PDF)
1. Corvus brachyrhynchos--Juvenile literature. I. Title.
QL696.P2367A466 2016
598.8′64--dc23   2015030134

Editorial Credits
Nikki Bruno Clapper, editor; Katelin Plekkenpol and Juliette Peters, designers;
Jo Miller, media researcher; Tori Abraham, production specialist

Photo Credits
Alamy: Doug McCutcheon, 13; Dreamstime: Brian Kushner, 5; Getty Images:
Science Source/Scott Camazine, 17, 19; Newscom: Design Pics/Robert L. Potts,
21; Shutterstock: Melinda Fawver, Cover (inset), 1 (inset) Paul Sparks, 9, Piotrf
Wawrzyniuk, Cover (background), 1 (background), 2-3, 24, SDanussa, flowers
(throughout), Steve Bower, 11, Steve Byland, 7; The Image Works: Tom Bushey, 15

Note to Parents and Teachers

The Backyard Birds set supports national curriculum standards for science related to
life science and ecosystems. This book describes and illustrates American crows. The
images support early readers in understanding the text. The repetition of words and
phrases helps early readers learn new words. This book also introduces early readers
to subject-specific vocabulary words, which are defined in the Glossary section. Early
readers may need assistance to read some words and to use the Table of Contents,
Glossary, Read More, Internet Sites, Critical Thinking Using the Common Core, and
Index sections of the book.

Printed in the United States   5820

Table of Contents

All About Crows 4
Where Crows Live 12
The Life of a Crow 16

Crow Range 22
Glossary 22
Read More 23
Internet Sites 23
Critical Thinking
    Using the Common Core 24
Index 24

All About Crows

Caw! Caw! Caw! This noisy bird is an American crow. These crows live in the United States and Canada.

An adult crow is 16 to 21 inches (41 to 53 centimeters) long. Crows are black all over. Even their legs and beaks are black.

Crows eat insects, small animals, seeds, and fruit. They also eat trash. Sometimes they steal food from other animals.

Crows are smart.
They use tools to dig
up food. Groups of crows
work together to chase
away predators.

Where Crows Live

American crows live in the United States and Canada. They live in cities, in backyards, and in the countryside.

Crows live in family groups. Each group has four to seven birds. In fall and winter they roost in flocks. Some flocks have 2 million crows!

The Life of a Crow

In spring a male and
a female crow build a nest.
The female crow lays three to
nine eggs. She sits on them
to keep them warm.

After about 17 days the chicks hatch. Parents feed the hungry chicks. About 35 days later, the chicks leave the nest.

Crows talk to each other.
Some calls mean "come"
or "stay away." Others mean
that food or danger is near.
Can you talk like a crow?

Crow Range

Summer

Year-round

Glossary

flock—a group of the same kind of animal; members of flocks live, travel, and eat together

hatch—to break out of an egg

insect—a small animal with a hard outer shell, six legs, three body sections, and two antennae; most insects have wings

predator—an animal that hunts other animals for food

roost—to settle in a place to rest

Read More

Martin, Isabel. *Birds: A Question and Answer Book.* Pebble Plus: Animal Kingdom Questions and Answers. North Mankato, Minn.: Capstone Press, 2015.

Otfinoski, Steven. *Crows.* Backyard Safari. New York: Cavendish Square Publishing, 2015.

Owen, Ruth. *Crows.* The World's Smartest Animals. New York: Windmill Books, 2012.

Internet Sites

FactHound offers a safe, fun way to find Internet sites related to this book. All of the sites on FactHound have been researched by our staff.

Here's all you do:

Visit *www.facthound.com*

Type in this code: 9781491485118

Check out projects, games and lots more at **www.capstonekids.com**

Critical Thinking
Using the Common Core

1. What is a predator? How do crows react to predators? (Craft and Structure)

2. What do crows look like? Why do you think some people are scared of crows? (Integration of Knowledge and Ideas)

3. Crows are really smart. Can you think of other animals that are smart? What are some things the animals do to show you they are smart? (Integration of Knowledge and Ideas)

Index

calls, 4, 20

colors, 6

eggs, 16

flocks, 14

food, 8, 10, 18, 20

habitats, 12

nests, 16, 18

predators, 10

range, 4, 12

size, 6

tools, 10

young, 18